CONGRATULATIONS, You're a PARENT!

Congratulations, You're a Parent!

13-Digit ISBN: 978-1-95151-169-2
10-Digit ISBN: 1-951511-69-7

This book may be ordered by mail from the publisher. Please include $5.99 for postage and handling.

Please support your local bookseller first!

Books published by Cider Mill Press Book Publishers are available at special discounts for bulk purchases in the United States by corporations, institutions, and other organizations. For more information, please contact the publisher.

Cider Mill Press Book Publishers
"Where good books are ready for press"
501 Nelson Place
Nashville, Tennessee 37214

cidermillpress.com

Typography: Acumin Pro, DoUbLeBaSs, Carrotflower

Printed in India

23 24 25 26 27 REP 5 4 3 2 1
First Edition

CONGRATULATIONS,
You're a PARENT!

Illustrated by Rhoda Domingo

CIDER MILL
PRESS

BOOK
PUBLISHERS

Congratulations,
you're a parent!

Welcome to parenthood, where everything goes according to plan.

Just kidding.

You never slept that great
to begin with, right?

Don't worry about changing diapers, babies only drink milk.

And speaking of milk,
it's only spilled milk!

But remember
to clean food
off the walls
before it dries.

Your home will be filled
with joy, laughter, and many,
many tripping hazards.

Privacy is overrated.

Think of all the
water you'll save
showering together!

It's a good thing you've always been able to ignore loud noises.

Remember how you once said you enjoyed doing laundry?

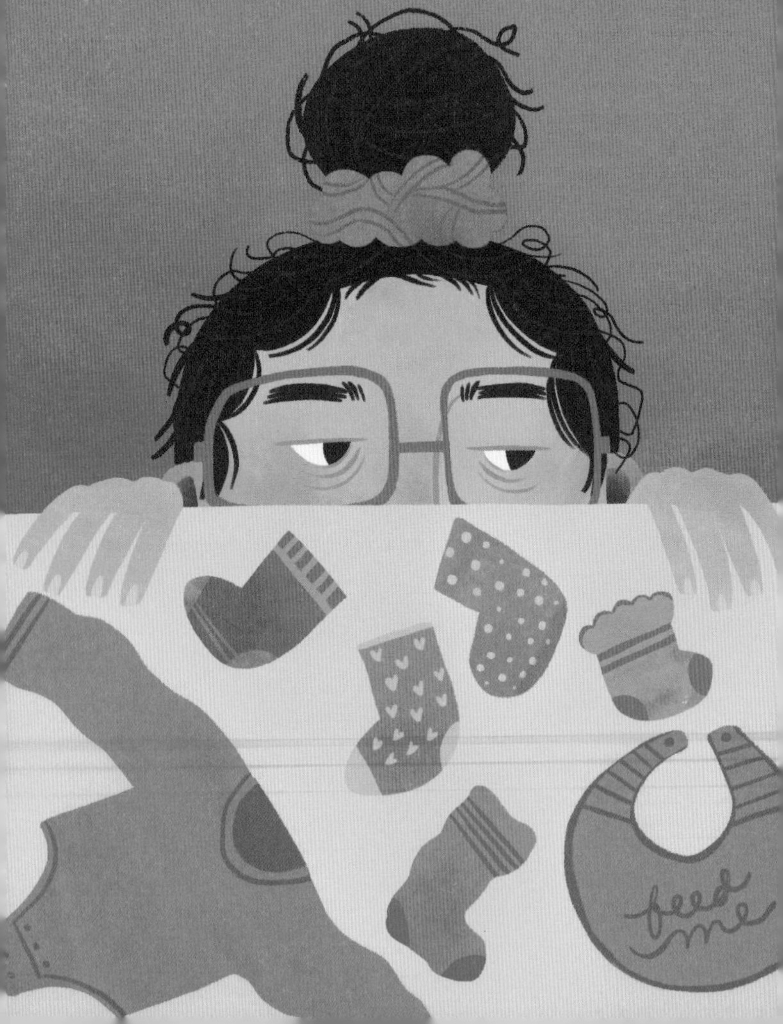

At least now you can really organize your books.

Now you have someone
to run errands with.

Always make the best
of your "me time."

Road trips
are the best.

Until they aren't . . . .

You weren't going to work from home forever, right?

Your immune system will be stronger than ever.

You've never needed
an excuse to add
to your wardrobe.

Every day is filled with
unexpected treasures!

Being a parent is the best!

About Cider Mill Press
Book Publishers

Good ideas ripen with time. From seed to harvest,
Cider Mill Press brings fine reading, information, and
entertainment together between the covers of its creatively
crafted books. Our Cider Mill bears fruit twice a year,
publishing a new crop of titles each spring and fall.

"Where Good Books Are Ready for Press"

501 Nelson Place
Nashville, Tennessee 37214

cidermillpress.com